World Almanac® Library of American Immigration

Italian Americans

Dale Anderson

Curriculum Consultant: Michael Koren,
Social Studies Teacher, Maple Dale School, Fox Point, Wisconsin

WORLD ALMANAC® LIBRARY

To Vincent and Mary Altomare, who came to America and taught their children —and grandchildren—the values of caring for family, working hard, and having fun.

Please visit our web site at: www.garethstevens.com
For a free color catalog describing World Almanac® Library's
list of high-quality books and multimedia programs,
call 1-800-848-2928 (USA) or 1-800-387-3178 (Canada).
World Almanac® Library's fax: (414) 332-3567.

Library of Congress Cataloging-in-Publication Data

Anderson, Dale, 1953–
      Italian Americans / by Dale Anderson.
            p. cm. – (World Almanac Library of American immigration)
      Includes bibliographical references and index.
      ISBN-10: 0-8368-7312-2 – ISBN-13: 978-0-8368-7312-2 (lib. bdg.)
      ISBN-10: 0-8368-7325-4 – ISBN-13: 978-0-8368-7325-2 (softcover)
      1. Italian Americans–History–Juvenile literature.   2. Italian Americans–
Social conditions–Juvenile literature.   3. Immigrants–United States–History–
Juvenile literature.   4. Italy–Emigration and immigration–History–Juvenile
literature.   5. United States–Emigration and immigration–History–Juvenile
literature. I. Title. II. Series.
      E184.I8A54   2007
      973'.00451–dc22   4388   2006005322

First published in 2007 by
World Almanac® Library
A member of the WRC Media Family of Companies
330 West Olive Street, Suite 100
Milwaukee, WI 53212, USA

Copyright © 2007 by World Almanac® Library.

Produced by Discovery Books
Editor: Sabrina Crewe
Designer and page production: Sabine Beaupré
Photo researcher: Sabrina Crewe
Maps and diagrams: Stefan Chabluk
Consultant: Maddalena Marinari
Gareth Stevens editorial direction: Mark J. Sachner
Gareth Stevens editor: Carol Ryback
Gareth Stevens art direction: Tammy West
Gareth Stevens production: Jessica Morris

Picture credits: CORBIS: title page, 27, 42, 43; Granger Collection: 13; Library
of Congress: 8, 9, 12, 17, 18, 20, 21, 22, 23, 24, 25, 26, 29, 30, 32, 36, 38, 39;
National Archives: 35; National Park Service: 15, 16, 19; New York Public Library:
cover, 4; U.S. Marine Corps: 34.

Printed in the United States of America

1 2 3 4 5 6 7 8 9 10 09 08 07 06

Contents

Front cover: An Italian American family gathers at the table for dinner in 1915. This family lived in New York City, where many Italian immigrants arrived between 1880 and 1924.

Title page: Every July, Italian Americans hold the *Festa del Giglio* in Brooklyn in New York City. The festival is a tradition brought to the United States many years ago by immigrants from Italy.

Introduction

T he United States has often been called "a nation of immigrants." With the exception of Native Americans—who have inhabited North America for thousands of years—all Americans can trace their roots to other parts of the world.

Immigration is not a thing of the past. While more than seventy million people came to the United States between 1820 and 2005, one-fifth of that total—about fourteen million people—immigrated since the start of 1990. Overall, more people have immigrated permanently to the United States than to any other single nation.

◀ Italian craftspeople are well known for their skill and artistry. This Italian American bronze worker was photographed in 1930.

Push and Pull

Historians write of the "push" and "pull" factors that lead people to emigrate. "Push" factors are the conditions in the homeland that convince people to leave. Many immigrants to the United States were—and still are—fleeing persecution or poverty. "Pull" factors are those that attract people to settle in another country. The dream of freedom, or jobs, or both, continues to pull immigrants to the United States. People from many countries around the world view the United States as a place of opportunity.

Building a Nation

Immigrants to the United States have not always found what they expected. People worked long hours for little pay, often doing jobs that others did not want to do. Many groups also endured prejudice.

In spite of these challenges, immigrants and their children built the United States of America, from its farms, railroads, and computer industries to its beliefs and traditions. They have enriched American life with their culture and ideas. Although they honor their heritage, most immigrants and their descendants are proud to call themselves Americans first and foremost.

The Italian American Contribution

In 1492, Italian sailor Christopher Columbus launched European settlement of the Americas. Another explorer from Italy had a lasting impact—America is named after Italian Amerigo Vespucci, who traveled to the Americas in about 1500 and was among the first European explorers to realize they had reached a new landmass.

"I have been an American for so long—fifty years—that I often forget I was born in Italy. . . . Once I went back to my native city and planned to stay there for a year or more. . . . What did I find? I was a foreigner in Italy. I could speak the language of course, but I couldn't think Italian. . . . I had planned to be away for a year, but in four months I was on my return trip to the Bronx."

Attilio Piccirilli, sculptor who came to the United States in 1888 at age twenty-two

Since those early journeys, nearly 5.5 million Italians have immigrated to the United States, making them one of the nation's largest immigrant groups in history. The vast majority—more than 4.6 million—came between 1881 and 1924.

Italian immigrants and their descendants have made many contributions to American life. Thousands helped build the nation or launched businesses—large and small—that gave jobs to many U.S. citizens. Italian Americans had a dramatic impact on life in New York City and in many other cities. The Italian dedication to family has put its stamp on life in the United States.

Life in
the Homeland

For many centuries, the land in southern Europe that is now Italy was cut into several separate states, some ruled by foreign powers. In the middle 1800s, several Italian leaders launched a movement to unite Italy. Northern regions united and took control of southern Italy and the island of Sicily. After much conflict, the kingdom of Italy was proclaimed in 1861.

The Village

Three major forces marked the culture of Italy, especially in the south. These forces were village, family, and church. They would have an impact on how Italian immigrants lived in the United States.

The village where people were born, lived, and died was the source of each person's identity. As Italian American professor and writer Richard Gambino explains: "Not only each region, but each town, feels itself a self-contained, unique culture, its people feeling no kinship with those even a few miles away." People from other villages were not trusted. Emigrants carried this *campanilismo*, or traditional sense of community, to the United States.

The Family

Family was even more important. If someone in the family was hurt, others rallied to support and protect him or her, even carrying out revenge against whoever caused the suffering. In 1877, Italy's government passed a law requiring all children to go to school. Many southern Italians ignored it, in part because parents worried that the teacher might undermine the moral lessons they taught at home.

The Church

The Catholic Church also played an important role in southern Italian life. Each village was proud of—and devoted to—its own patron saint. People were deeply religious, but most Italian men went to church only for family weddings and baptisms.

Church officials were not entirely trusted—when people needed help, they rarely went to the priest but prayed to Mary, the mother of Jesus, and to their patron saints. Many also believed in evil spirits and magical powers that the church and its priests had no control over. Bad fortune could result from a neighbor's curse on a person, a family, or crops.

Regional Differences

The political conflicts of the mid-1800s caused some emigration to the United States. About twenty thousand Italians arrived in the United States between 1851 and 1870. After Italy was unified, however, it faced more problems. Most southern Italians saw themselves as belonging to their region, not to Italy. They were, for instance, *Abruzzese* from Abruzzi or *Calabrese* from Calabria. Each region had a unique culture and its own dialect. One cause of tension between northern and southern Italians was that, because of different dialects, they could not really speak to each other. Italy's national government was dominated by northern Italians, who passed laws and introduced high taxes that hit southern Italy harshly.

Poverty and Disasters

In addition, most people in southern Italy were poor. Much of the land was in the hands of large landowners, and poor people farmed that land, working long hours for low pay. Their food was bread, lentils, or beans, and sometimes cheese. The lucky few might eat meat twice a year, at Christmas and at Easter. Their homes were

▲ Italy, in southern Europe, has a mostly warm and dry Mediterranean climate. The southern part of the country includes the large island of Sicily, from which many emigrants left for the United States.

▲ Poor rural Italians in the late 1800s and early 1900s farmed fields belonging to rich landowners. They had little opportunity to improve their lives.

huts with dirt floors and no furniture. Natural disasters added to the misery. Severe, recurring droughts at the end of the 1800s caused crops to fail. In 1906, Mount Vesuvius, in one of its frequent volcanic eruptions, killed more than one hundred people. Two years later, an earthquake caused a huge tsunami that swept over the coasts of Italy, killing nearly two hundred thousand people.

> "In them days, there was two classes of people in Sicily: the rich and the very poor. My family was very poor. I never went to school. I started working from before I was ten years old. My father and mother, they send me to work to make maybe ten cents a day. . . . I work from one o'clock in the morning to about two in the afternoon the next day. . . . Them days, if you make ten cents a day, that was a lot of money."
>
> *Peter Mossini, who came to the United States in 1921 and settled in western Pennsylvania*

Reasons to Leave

Poverty and disasters caused several million people to emigrate from Italy from 1880 through the 1920s. One man summed up the reasoning that led many people to choose to leave. He said, "When I found that the only way I could prevent my family from starving was to turn to stealing, I decided it was time to leave."

The flood of emigrants from Italy slowed in the 1920s and 1930s. In those years, the U.S. government introduced severe limits on immigration from certain nations in Europe, including Italy.

The Impact of Emigration

Many towns in southern Italy lost many people because of emigration to the United States. In the region of Calabria, nearly one-third of all families were without a male head of household. Some single men who remained in Italy demanded higher dowries than had been typical before. They knew that, with so few men left in southern Italy, they were in high demand. For these reasons, many young women who wanted to get married never could.

Some communities benefited, however. Emigrants sent money back to their families in Italy, and that money was used to build new homes called *case Americane*, or American houses. Some local economies flourished, and emigrant money flowing from the United States helped boost Italy's national economy.

World War II kept emigration slow in the 1940s. After the war, there was a new surge in emigration to the United States. A few thousand emigrants were war brides—Italian women who married U.S. soldiers. Most postwar emigrants left to seek work because the economy of southern Italy was poor once again. The Italian government urged the United States and other nations to accept large numbers of Italian immigrants. The United States passed a law that allowed up to four hundred thousand people displaced by the war in Italy and other countries to come to the United States.

These factors helped produce a rise in Italian emigration to the United States that continued up to about 1970. After that time, the United States ceased to be the main destination for Italians, who headed instead for other parts of Europe.

Today, only two or three thousand people come from Italy to the United States each year. They come for a variety of reasons. Some join other family members already here. Others are looking for better opportunities or a different way of life.

▶ A group of homeless Italians, refugees from an earthquake, prepares to leave Italy for the United States in the early 1900s.

CHAPTER 2

Emigration

hile life in Italy was hard, the decision to leave was not easy. With their intense ties to village and family, Italians who chose to journey to what they called *"LaMerica"* were taking themselves away from what they valued most. Also, most rural Italians had never set foot outside their home village. For them, crossing an ocean must have seemed a huge challenge. During the years from 1881 to the early 1920s, several million Italians faced many of the same emigration experiences.

Mostly Men

The vast majority of people who left Italy between 1881 and 1924 were men of working age who planned to return to Italy. For a time, males outnumbered females three to one. Over time, many of these men—husbands and fathers—sent for their wives and children to join them. Older male children sometimes joined their fathers first so they could help earn the money to buy tickets for the rest of the family. After about 1900, an increasing proportion of Italian immigrants were women. Larger numbers were children, too, but there were still fewer children from Italy than from other countries.

The Ritornati

Most Italians who emigrated to the United States between 1881 and 1924 did not intend to stay. Large numbers returned to Italy after earning enough money to buy land, usually within five years of their coming. The number of these *ritornati*, or returning emigrants, is estimated to be anywhere from one-third to one-half of those who went to the United States in certain years. Some went back and forth more than once. Many Italian immigrants, however, decided finally to stay and make their home in the United States, even if they had originally planned to return to Italy.

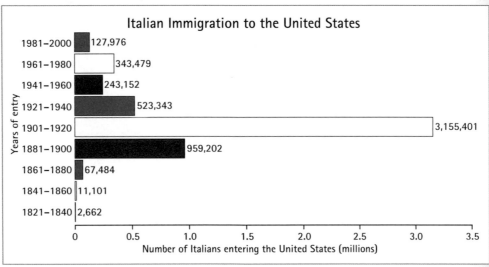

Italian Immigration to the United States

Years of entry	Number of Italians entering the United States (millions)
1981–2000	127,976
1961–1980	343,479
1941–1960	243,152
1921–1940	523,343
1901–1920	3,155,401
1881–1900	959,202
1861–1880	67,484
1841–1860	11,101
1821–1840	2,662

Source: U.S. Citizenship and Immigration Services, 1821–2000

▲ This chart shows the number of Italians who came to the United States in twenty-year periods between 1821 and 2000. More than three million came in the peak years between 1901 and 1920. Some of them returned to Italy after a few years. In 2000, an estimated ten thousand Italians were living illegally—with neither citizenship nor temporary status—in the United States.

Problems of Separation

While fathers toiled in the United States to earn the passage money, those left behind faced many difficulties. One of the worst was not hearing any word. People did not have telephones, and the only way of getting news was by mail. Men sent letters when they could, but that was not very often. When letters did arrive in Italy, they were greeted with joy.

Problems did not always end when a man sent word that he wanted his wife and children to join him in the United States. Wives had to go through the terrifying process of emigration to a faraway country despite the fact that they had probably never left their villages before in their lives. Some wives just refused to go.

Another difficulty was that of saying good-bye. Fathers who

"My father . . . came to America [first]. . . . We were supposed to come to this country in 1907, two years before we finally did. My father sent cash to my mother to buy the boat tickets. But my grandfather fell off a horse and got sick. My mother spent the money on doctors. . . . In 1909, the year we came, my father got smart. He sent no cash, just the paid tickets."

Mario Vina, who came to the United States in 1909 and settled with his family in Connecticut

▲ An early photograph shows the harbor at Naples, Italy, where most Italians embarked on ships that would carry them across the Atlantic Ocean to the United States. Many others left from Genoa or from Palermo, on the island of Sicily.

went alone faced the sorrow of leaving their wives and children. Even when the whole family traveled, they had to say good-bye to grandparents, aunts, uncles, and cousins. These departures were often painful, both for emigrants and for those left behind.

"We stayed with my Grandmom [before leaving Italy] and, oh God bless her, she just cried and cried. She lost two daughters and three grandchildren all at once. And she just kept crying and crying. . . . Now that I'm a grandmother, if I would lose [my daughter] and three grandchildren—can you imagine the hurt? . . . And grandfather . . . oh, the tears and the tears when we left."

Rosa Bolognese DaDamio, who came to the United States with her family in 1920

The Journey

The first step of the journey was to find a way to Naples or Palermo, the main Italian ports from which steamships left for the United States. With no cars and few trains, many people traveled in wagons or on foot.

Then came an ocean voyage that lasted a week or two, depending on the speed of the ship and the weather it encountered. Conditions in steerage class were awful. Males and females were placed in separate areas, splitting families. There was little fresh air. Furnishings were limited to bunk beds. Large numbers of people—some ill and some made seasick by the rolling of the ship—shared one toilet. When steerage passengers came up

"Then, on that boat, the people lived like animals. It was big, like a cellar. The beds . . . were all on top [of] each other. . . . There was no dining room. They just go outside of the boat and sit there. No chairs, the people sit on the floor. I was scared. . . . And I was sick. We take about twelve days. Yeah. I was sick all the time. I don't eat nothing."

Maria Prioriello Battisti, who came to Pennsylvania in 1923

onto the deck during the day, they were usually confined to the area behind the ship's smoke-stacks, where the air was dirty and smoky.

The food was poor. Later travelers ate better than earlier ones. Warned by letters from the United States that the food on board the ship would be bad, they brought bread, salami, cheese, and other supplies with them.

Later Travelers

Another four hundred thousand Italians emigrated to the United States between 1951 and 1970, forming a large second wave. Immigrants who came after 1950 found a different route across the Atlantic. Italy—even the poor parts of southern Italy—was no longer a region of mule-drawn carts and foot travel, and steamships no longer crossed the Atlantic Ocean in large numbers. These migrants used modern transporta-tion systems in Italy and flew across the ocean. One son of the first wave of immigrants remem-bers that he and his family called the later arrivals "immi-grants with wings."

▶ A photograph from 1900 shows the deck of a ship crowded with Italian immigrants who had just made the diffi-cult crossing from Italy. Many people arrived sick and hungry.

CHAPTER 3

Arriving in the United States

Before 1880, immigrants from Italy came in small numbers. Some were welcomed for their skills, such as glassblowers from Venice who came to Virginia in the early 1600s, or stonecutters who later settled in Vermont. Others were exiles, sent out of Italy because of their political activities. The 1850 Census showed 3,465 people of Italian birth living in the United States.

The Island of Tears

After 1880, this number changed dramatically. Between 1881 and 1924, a total of 27.5 million people came to the United States, and one in every six was from Italy. The immigrants of this period—Italians and others—faced a bewildering experience on arrival.

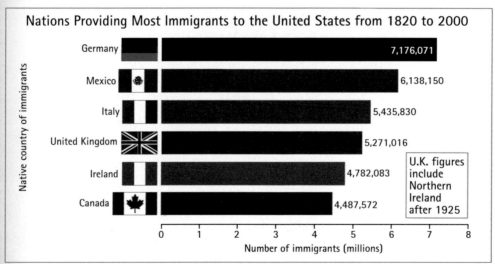

Source: U.S. Citizenship and Immigration Services, 1820–2000

▲ The nations that have provided the most immigrants to the United States are shown in this chart. More people have come from Italy than from any other nations except Germany and Mexico.

From 1892 to 1932, Ellis Island in New York Harbor was the U.S. government's main immigration station. Italian immigrants called Ellis Island *L'Isola delle Lagrime* (the Island of Tears).

The Medical Exam

On arrival in New York Harbor, steamships were met by smaller boats that took steerage passengers to Ellis Island to be processed. First, immigrants went through a medical inspection. Anyone who failed the inspection was sent back to Italy. Only around 2 percent of all immigrants were sent back, but this stage in the process still made immigrants very anxious.

Military doctors quickly looked over the immigrants to spot any obvious physical issues. They used chalk to write code letters on the clothing of any person with a problem. "B" meant a bad back, "FT" a foot problem, "H" a heart condition. Using a hook, they pulled up each person's eyelid to look for the signs of trachoma, an eye disease. This disease was grounds for being sent back.

About half the immigrants received no mark and passed on. The other half had to go to special rooms where they were examined more closely to determine the seriousness of the condition. If the doctors found the injury or sickness too severe, the person was sent back to Italy. Immigrants with curable illnesses were taken to the station's hospital and held until they were well. Angelina Palmiero,

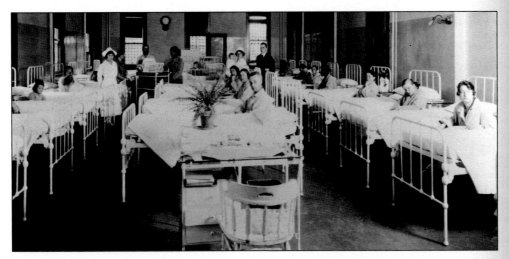

▲ People who were too sick to be admitted into the United States were either sent back to their own countries or detained in the Ellis Island hospital until they were better. Over the years, the hospital saved many lives. This photograph shows a women's ward on the island.

"This doctor and the nurses . . . were standing on the steps. And they would watch people, because there were such hordes of people, they didn't have time to examine each and every one. Just by the looks of them, they would pull people out from the crowd, and then they would examine them. But we came through without any problem at all. . . . We were lucky. There were many that were sent back."

Regina Rogatta, who reached Ellis Island in 1928

who arrived in 1923 at age ten, was sick with swollen glands. She was placed in the Ellis Island hospital. It was very hard on her: "Nobody told me anything. Nobody explained. . . . At night . . . [I would] go look out to the water and see the boats and the Statue of Liberty." After twenty-three days, she finally rejoined her family.

Registry

Next, hopeful immigrants registered with an immigration agent. The names and ages of all the immigrants were recorded in huge registry books. Officials asked immigrants where in the United States they were going and what relative, if any, they were joining. Immigrants declared their occupations and how much cash they were carrying. Interpreters translated the agents' questions and the immigrants' answers.

It has often been claimed that immigration officials changed the names of new arrivals to make them more "American." Some historians, however, say any changes may have been errors. Either way, some immigrants found their last names changed, with "Buonomo" becoming "Buono" and "Benedetto" turning into "Bennett." After leaving Ellis Island, other immigrants decided to change their names. They did so in the hopes of having an easier life if their Italian origins were unknown.

▲ People wait to be interviewed by immigration officials in the large registry room on Ellis Island. For some, the process was quick. Others waited many hours or even days.

Problems with Entry

The entire process could take very little time—under an hour for an immigrant who experienced no difficulties. The atmosphere was tense, however. The huge registry room filled with hundreds of immigrants at a time. Tired and anxious about what would happen next, people clutched their bundles of belongings. Most moved through quickly, but some were taken out of line because of illness, misunderstanding, or other problems. Sometimes, children were taken away—perhaps for examination—and this of course frightened parents who could not understand what was happening.

In 1917, the U.S. Congress passed a law requiring that immigrants pass a literacy test. Some poorer Italians could not read and write, and so they could be barred from entering. People could also be

▲ An Italian mother with young children and a bundle of belongings arrives at Ellis Island to start a new life in 1910.

Aliens and Citizens

In the period between 1880 and 1920, Italians and other immigrants approved for entry became resident aliens. They were not citizens, but they had the right to live and work in the United States. They also had rights under the U.S. Constitution, such as freedom of speech and religion. After five years, white resident aliens could apply to become citizens. The process of becoming a U.S. citizen through residency is known as naturalization. People had to be of "good moral character" and had to swear allegiance to the United States. After 1906, they were also required to speak English. From 1855 until 1922, women were able to acquire U.S. citizenship without naturalization if they were married to a U.S. citizen. Children also acquired citizenship automatically through their parents. Children born in the United States were awarded citizenship at birth, even if their parents were resident aliens.

excluded if they had no money or if there were no relatives or friends to take responsibility for them.

It was always a relief when the agent approved entry. Then the immigrants passed through the far end of the registry room and began the next stage of their journey. Often family members were there to greet them. Mario Vina, who came through Ellis Island in 1909, remembers rejoining his father: "All of a sudden, my mother spotted him, spotted my father. She says, 'It's Papa!' I looked. I had forgotten what he looked like, you know. My mother hugged him, kissed him. He hugged me and patted me on the back." Similar reunions took place hundreds of times every day.

First Steps in a New Land

Farming was what this first wave of Italian immigrants had known. Few could farm in the United States, however, because they did not have the cash to buy land. Most Italian immigrants, therefore, settled first in large cities where they could find jobs. Many stayed in and near New York City, where they had landed. By 1920, New York City was home to four hundred thousand Italian Americans. Many moved to what came to be called "Little Italy" in lower Manhattan. Italian immigrants also moved into the city's other four boroughs: the Bronx, Brooklyn, Queens, and Staten Island.

▼ Mulberry Street, shown here in about 1900, was and still is the heart of New York City's "Little Italy." Many thousands of Italians and other immigrants from southern and eastern Europe came to settle in the district when they first arrived.

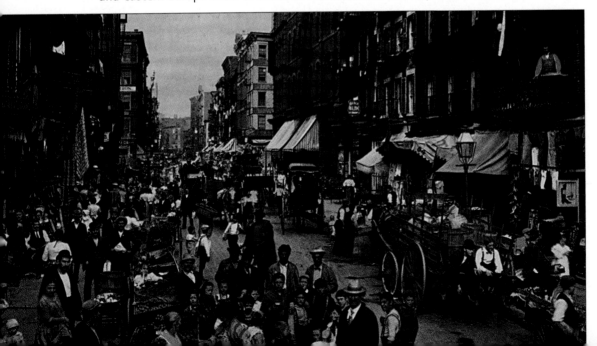

Spreading Out
Other newly arrived Italians fanned out to the states of New England and the mid-Atlantic region. These areas had large cities with growing industries, and those industries needed workers. Philadelphia had more than seventy-five thousand Italian Americans by 1910. Italian immigrants in Boston moved into the area called the North End, pushing out Irish and German Americans who had arrived decades before. Many Italian immigrants also settled in Pittsburgh, Pennsylvania. In the Midwest, meanwhile, Chicago, Illinois; Detroit, Michigan; and Cleveland, Ohio, also attracted immigrants.

▲ The later wave of immigrants, arriving by airplane over New York City, saw a sight that had greeted generations of immigrants since the 1880s. To many, the Statue of Liberty in New York Harbor symbolized the new life they were about to begin.

Some Italians went as far as the West Coast. At one time, Italian Americans made up the largest foreign-born population of California. There, many immigrants from northern Italy made their living by farming. Few Italians went to the southern states, but there was a sizable Italian American population in New Orleans, Louisiana, and a pocket of several hundred in Bryan, Texas.

The Later Wave
The great majority of the later wave—those who arrived after 1950—settled on the East Coast. About one-third of them moved to New York City. Some of the newer immigrants found it easier to settle into American life than those who came in the great wave before them. This was, in part, because groups such as the Roman Catholic Church took steps to help them adjust.

Building Communities

I talian immigrants from the 1880s to the 1920s faced poverty, hard work, prejudice, and unfair treatment. They had to build new lives in a very different world.

Village Neighborhoods

Italian Americans coming from small villages had to adjust to life in huge, noisy, bustling cities. While some cities had an Italian section, a "Little Italy," most cities had several areas where Italians lived.

Early Italian Americans

The first Italian Americans, those that came before 1880, had different experiences from those of the great wave described in this chapter. Earlier immigrants were mostly from northern Italy, and many were artists and craftspeople. Teacher and philosopher Philip Mazzei came to Virginia before the American Revolution, where he became a friend of Thomas Jefferson. In 1774, he wrote an essay stating that "All men are by nature equally free and independent." That essay may have influenced Jefferson in writing the Declaration of Independence. Three units of Italian Americans fought for independence in the American Revolution, and many Italian Americans fought for the Union during the American Civil War. Lorenzo da Ponte helped oversee the building of the first U.S. opera house. In the mid-1850s, Constantino Brumidi painted several scenes from U.S. history inside the U.S. Capitol.

⌃ Constantino Brumidi painted a huge fresco, part of it shown above, on the ceiling of the Rotunda in the U.S. Capitol.

What sharply marked Italian American settlement was that people from one village often settled in the same neighborhood, town, or city. Many families from one Sicilian village, Valledolmo, all turned up in the same town, Fredonia, in New York. In large cities, different villages settled in different neighborhoods. One historian traced seventeen such clusters in Chicago, Illinois. About half of all the Italians in Cleveland, Ohio, came from the same ten villages.

Chain Migration

These patterns resulted not from plan but from the process of immigration. Italian immigration followed a pattern called chain migration, in which one member of a family would come to the United States to earn money to buy passage for others. When they sent for brothers or spouses, the new arrivals naturally settled in the same neighborhood. Other cousins or friends from the same village who came to the United States would move to that neighborhood, too. Over time, more and more people from the same village ended up in the same neighborhood.

The Padrone System

Some Italian Americans saw opportunity in the mass migration of Italians to the United States. They took on the role of a labor contractor, or *padrone* (a combination of patron and employer). The padrone agreed to pay the cost of travel and to get the immigrant a job. The immigrant agreed to pay part of his wages to the padrone.

In 1885, the U.S. government passed a law banning these agreements, but the padrone system continued to operate. By the early

▼ A padrone supervises Italian American workers picking cranberries in New Jersey.

1900s, however, the padrone system became less necessary. As more and more Italians settled in the United States, they arranged work for their arriving relatives.

Laborers and Storekeepers

Trained carpenters or masons were able to make a living from their skills. Most Italian immigrants, however, had worked on farms and had few nonagricultural skills. They hired out their muscles, working as manual laborers wherever they could. About four thousand Sicilians who had settled in New York City dug the tunnels that became one of the city's subway lines. Hundreds more swept the city's streets every day. In Philadelphia, Pennsylvania, Italian Americans built roads, railroads, and subways in the city. In the Midwest, men labored in factories that made steel, cars, and other products.

▲ A street vendor sells clams from his pushcart in New York City's Italian district in the early 1900s. The *farmacia* (pharmacy) next to the pushcart is also an Italian business.

Italian Americans also opened small stores, where they made pasta or sold produce and Italian foods to the people in the neighborhood. Those who could not afford to buy or rent a space for a store might build a pushcart. They loaded their carts with fresh fruit and vegetables or other goods each morning and then pushed the cart along the city's streets until they had sold out.

Women and Children

As families tried to make their way in their new homes, everyone worked. Women did all the cooking and cleaning, but many worked outside the home as well. Nobody could afford to overlook any possible source of income. Many did sewing or similar work at home each night, earning pennies for each piece of work that they finished. Others worked at clothing or cigar factories.

Even young children worked to help the family survive. If laws required them to be in school, they simply told the principal that their family was moving to another school district. Only a tiny fraction of the early arrivals went as far as high school. In New York City in 1920, about 90 percent of Italian American girls over age fourteen worked. If there were small children, the oldest girl—from as young as age ten—cared for them. Once that daughter reached fourteen, she, too, got a job outside the home.

"My first job was [in] a pants factory where they made . . . pants . . . for the American soldier. . . . And I worked on the second floor there, pressing certain bits of trousers. I was fourteen but I lied. I told them I was sixteen, and I know they didn't believe me, but I got twenty-five cents an hour, twelve dollars a week. That was big money for my family. . . . Whenever we got our salary we took the whole darn thing home."

Charles Carabello, who lived in Reading, Pennsylvania, with his Italian American family

▲ These Italian American boys, all eleven years old, were photographed in 1910 selling newspapers late on a winter's night in Buffalo, New York. Everyone in immigrant families worked hard to provide enough money for food and shelter.

◀ Italian American fishermen gather to discuss the day's news on Fisherman's Wharf, San Francisco. Italian American families were at the heart of the West Coast fishing industry for many years.

Farming and Fishing in the West

Life was different for Italian Americans who moved to California. Settlement by immigrants had come later there than on the East Coast. Italians who settled on the West Coast, therefore, did not have to compete so strongly with earlier groups of immigrants for jobs and land.

While some Italians settled in coastal cities (San Francisco, California, had a large Italian American community), many also started farms. Others became pioneers in the state's infant wine industry. Others grew fruit and vegetables. Along the coast, fishermen from Sicily and Genoa worked hard to build California's fishing industry.

Family Life

One big change for Italian Americans was the lack of extended family. In Italy, the grandfather was the head of the family, and the grandmother was looked up to as well. This older generation rarely made the crossing, however, and so parents and children did not have some of the resources they had known in the homeland. Groups called mutual aid societies helped fill some of the gaps, such as watching young children while the mother worked. Part of

"You know, in those days, the family come to propose, not the boy. Yes, the family come. You know, 'My son wants to marry your daughter.' 'Okay.' And it was no problem for us, because we thought that's the way it was supposed to be. They used to match them up, sort of. . . . A couple of them I says . . . 'Ma, I don't like him. You're not going to marry him; I am. You want him? You marry him.' I wouldn't marry anybody if I didn't like him."

Grace Calabrese, who came to the United States in 1924 and lived in New York City

"We rented two rooms in an old house and bought some furniture from a young couple who were moving out. They sold us a little stove and four chairs and a table and a few pots and pans and a bed for my mother and dad. First my brother and I slept on the floor, and then they bought a couple of little folding cots for us. We slept in the kitchen and mother and father in the other room. That's all we had for about ten years."

Joseph Baccardo, who came to the United States in 1898 and settled near Philadelphia

▾ For many Italian American mothers, their dark, cramped apartments were also their workplaces. At home with small children, they sewed clothes for the garment industry. Many other women worked in factories.

the traditional system of family ties, however, was lost.

Some family traditions continued. Families gathered on Sunday, often at the parents' home, to share a family meal. Larger gatherings that included aunts, uncles, and cousins took place throughout the year. The father was still viewed as the authority figure in the home, and children were expected to do as they were told. Families arranged marriages—they were not matters of choice for the couple.

Housing

Immigrant housing in the late 1800s and early 1900s was usually awful. Many tenement buildings were poorly built and had few windows to let in fresh air and light. Large families were crowded into small apartments. In 1904, officials in Philadelphia, Pennsylvania, found there was only one bathroom for every twenty-two families and one tub for more than one hundred people.

Learning the Language

Many female Italian immigrants never learned English. Living in Italian neighborhoods, they were able to speak their own language to neighbors and storekeepers. Even Italian American women who had jobs outside the home often worked in the community.

The situation was somewhat different for men, whose work more often took them outside the neighborhood. They learned as much English as they needed to in order to get by. At home, however, the immigrant generation typically spoke Italian.

Children often find it easier to acquire a new language than adults, and Italian children learned English faster than their parents. Some of the children attended school for at least a few years before they reached working age, which also helped their English.

Facing Prejudice

Italian immigrants often faced prejudice. One Italian American recalled that her mother was pelted by snowballs thrown by American children whenever she went shopping. Some signs of prejudice were stronger. Italian Americans were called horrible names and treated as though they were stupid. Bosses cheated them if they thought they could get away with it. Apartment building owners often refused to rent rooms to Italian Americans. Fights erupted between Italian Americans and other groups, especially the Irish.

The worst violence took place in New Orleans, Louisiana, in 1891. The city was full of strong anti-Italian feeling, which was partly fueled by the police department's habit of blaming unsolved crimes on "unknown Sicilians." In 1890, the city's police

▼ New Orleans was home to one of the earliest communities of Italian Americans. This photograph shows the Italian neighborhood in New Orleans in about 1906.

chief was murdered, and the crime was blamed on some Italian Americans who had nothing to do with it. The accused men were eventually found not guilty. Before they could be released, a mob rushed into the prison where the men were held and brutally murdered them. Similar unjust executions happened elsewhere in the South over the next two decades.

Even when they were not being attacked or taken advantage of, Italian Americans were not treated with respect. As one later recalled, "We came to America in search of bread and felt the inferiority of beggars. Everything about us—our behavior, our diet, our [hesitant], uncertain speech—was interpreted in terms of that inferiority." Italian Americans, in turn, remained suspicious of people from other groups.

Forming Groups

From the start, Italian Americans formed groups to help one another live in their new homeland. One of the first was the Order of the Sons of Italy, founded in 1905. It aimed to help immigrants with money, housing, and education as they got settled in the United States. Within about fifteen years, the group grew to have thirteen hundred local branches and about 125,000 members. This group and others also worked to improve the image of Italian Americans in newspapers and other media.

People in many towns and cities joined mutual aid societies. By 1915, there were as many as three thousand of these groups. Some of them helped people from just one region, with one for people from Abruzzi and another for those who came from Sicily.

Two Roman Catholic groups led two of the aid efforts. The San Raffaele Society set up schools, hospitals, and shelter in fourteen states. The other effort was led by Mother Frances Xavier Cabrini,

▲ Mother Cabrini devoted her life to helping Italian Americans and other immigrants and poor people. She died in 1917 and was declared a saint by the Catholic Church in 1946.

who set up hospitals, orphanages, schools, and nurseries in North and South America. Mother Cabrini was herself an Italian immigrant.

Italian Americans and the Roman Catholic Church

Although the Roman Catholic Church took some steps to help immigrants, Italian Americans mistrusted the institution. Irish Americans dominated the Roman Church and viewed the Church and religion differently from the Italians. The two views clashed—many priests did not treat Italian Americans well, and Italian churchgoers responded with hostility toward the priests.

After 1899, church leaders in the United States began to introduce Italian parishes, and the situation improved. In 1918, about one-third of all the Italian Americans in New York City regularly went to church, although attendance was higher for church holidays.

Celebrating the Saints

Italian Americans continued one important religious tradition. In Italy, each village had a special festival to celebrate its patron saint. These *festas,* or feast days, were times of great celebration, when the whole town would turn out and parade statues of the saint and the Virgin Mary through the streets. Some festas lasted more than one day, and they were celebrated with music and food.

The festas were kept alive in the United States. Different neighborhoods celebrated different feast days, depending on which town or village in Italy the people were from. In New York City, San Gennaro—the patron saint of Naples—was celebrated in lower Manhattan. Another Manhattan neighborhood celebrated the feast of San Gandolfo, patron of a Sicilian town. One Brooklyn neighborhood, settled by the people of Nola, held the feast of San Paulino. In another Brooklyn neighborhood, people from Palermo celebrated Santa Rosalia.

"Their aromas of food, the sight of burly men swaying from side to side and lurching forward under the weight of enormous statues of . . . madonnas and saints laden with money and gifts, the music of the Italian bands in uniforms with dark-peaked caps, white shirts, and black ties and the bright arches of colored lights spanning the city streets are essential memories of my childhood."

Writer and professor Richard Gambino, on the religious festivals he saw in New York City as a child

Newspapers and Culture

Italian Americans maintained their traditions through newspapers and cultural activities. Wherever Italians settled, Italian language newspapers soon appeared. One of the longest lasting was *Il Progresso Italo-Americano*, published originally in 1880 in New York City. By 1920, the paper was selling 127,000 copies each week. Other papers sprang up in Chicago, Illinois; New Orleans, Louisiana; and Philadelphia, Pennsylvania. At first, like the mutual aid societies, many newspapers were aimed at people from a particular region of Italy.

Italian Americans also kept alive their love of opera, a very popular art form in Italy. Families saved to buy the earliest record players and their favorite recordings of Italian opera singers. Enrico Caruso, born in Italy, was a major star at New York City's Metropolitan Opera House in the early 1900s. He was wildly popular in Italian American homes. In 1931, the Metropolitan Opera launched weekly live broadcasts of its productions. Italian Americans flocked to their radios to hear their favorite musical works.

Also hugely popular in the early 1900s was a performer named Eduardo Migilaccio, who took the name of Farfariello. His performances included songs, dances, and comic sketches that made fun of the immigrants and their struggles adapting to life in the United States. He also sang popular Italian songs.

A 1911 edition of *Il Progresso Italo-Americano* headlines a story about a fire at the Triangle Shirtwaist Factory. Almost 150 employees died in the fire. Most of them were young immigrant women working in terrible conditions for little pay.

CHAPTER 5

Conflict and Adaptation

U p to the 1940s and 1950s, Italian Americans faced many conflicts in their new country. Over time, however, they grew to accept U.S. life, and other Americans grew to accept them. Older people found the adaptation the most difficult, while children found it easier to become American.

Backlash

The huge increase in immigration from 1880 to 1920 led to a backlash. This was not the first time that native-born Americans had complained that immigrants were hurting the country. The same

▼ A cartoon published in an 1891 magazine expresses the anti-immigrant feeling of the times. Arriving immigrants, representing everything feared by nativists, crowd at the feet of Uncle Sam.

Crime—Myths and Reality

Throughout the history of the United States, various immigrant groups have been blamed for increases in criminal activities. Chances are, this will continue as long as the U.S. welcomes any immigrants. Some of the prejudice against Italian Americans probably arose from an image of southern Italian immigrants stereotyped as lawless bandits and criminals—a myth that persisted into modern times, based on the activities of a few high-profile criminals.

For instance, in the early 1900s, an Italian American criminal movement called the Black Hand increased anti-immigrant prejudice. Its name came from the handprints of coal dust left on doorways as warnings to innocent people. Black Handers used terror tactics to frighten law-abiding people, mostly other immigrants, into paying them money. The Black Hand faded by the early 1920s.

After World War I (1914–1918), groups of gangsters gained control over criminal activities in large cities. Some of the most famous gangsters, such as Al Capone, were Italian Americans.

Most of the myths about Italian American crime today center around the Mafia, supposedly a network of families who gain wealth from extortion, gambling, and drug dealing. Some of the stories are true. There is a criminal organization in Sicily called the Mafia. During the 1900s, some Italian Americans became involved in crime and built strong organizations to carry out their activities. Competing organizations sometimes fought each other for control of an area. Several of the more sensational claims about the U.S. Mafia are not true, however. Families from different cities are not joined together in a vast criminal conspiracy that covers the nation, nor are Italian American criminal groups connected to Sicily's Mafia.

thing had happened in the mid-1800s, when a political party called the Know-Nothings opposed Irish immigration. Similar responses have arisen with other immigrant groups in recent years.

Many forces combined in the late 1800s to promote a new nativist movement. Protestants feared that growing numbers of Italian immigrants would increase the power of the Roman Catholic Church. Prejudice was also a factor. Many news stories and books charged that Italian immigrants were violent people, always ready to fight, and intent on revenge. The struggle for jobs was an issue, too. Groups that had arrived before, such as Irish Americans,

▲ A class of hopeful Italian Americans receives instruction in the English language and U.S. citizenship in New Jersey in the 1920s. As the door to immigration closed and quotas were enforced, U.S. citizenship became a prize for immigrants.

Serving Their Country

In the early 1900s, when many critics questioned the loyalty of immigrants to their new country, Italian Americans showed that these charges were groundless. About five hundred thousand immigrants served in the U.S. Army when, in 1917 and 1918, the United States was involved in World War I. Estimates say that as many as half the immigrants were of Italian descent. Italian Americans made up about 10 percent of the Army even though they represented only about 4 percent of the U.S. population.

grew angry when they saw recent Italian immigrants getting work that had once gone to them.

In 1920, a sensational crime captured the nation's attention. Nicola Sacco and Bartolomeo Vanzetti were falsely arrested for robbery and murder. The jury—in an unfair trial—found the two men guilty. The defense attorneys appealed the case, but the convictions were upheld. The Sacco and Vanzetti case helped increase other Americans' fear of immigrants, especially Italians. It helped convince many in Congress to vote for the laws limiting immigration. In 1927, the two men were executed.

Closing the Door

In 1921, Congress passed a law that put a limit on the number of immigrants allowed into the country. It also set up quotas for the number of immigrants allowed in from each nation. Congress based its quotas on the proportion of people from each country who already lived in the United States in 1920. This rule meant more English, Irish, and German immigrants would be allowed in than Italian or Jewish immigrants.

In 1924, Congress passed the National Origins Act. It dropped the total immigration limit even further. It also based the quotas for each national group on the nationality of those already living in the United States by 1890—at that time, the proportion of immigrants from Italy and eastern Europe had been even smaller than in 1920. This part of the law had a clear goal: Congress wanted to block further immigration from Italy and from eastern Europe. Supporters of the law pointed out that it would cut the number of Italians allowed into the country from forty thousand people a year to just four thousand people.

The 1924 National Origins Act had the desired impact on Italian immigration. More than 2 million Italians came to the United States from 1901 to 1910, and another 1.1 million came from 1911 to 1920. From 1921 to 1930, the number dropped to 455,315, most of whom came in the years before the quotas took hold. In the 1930s, the number fell to fewer than seventy thousand.

> "Our very existence is threatened. American institutions are threatened by this influx of the refuse and criminal hordes of foreign countries. Some time ago the chairman of the Committee on Immigration in the House . . . said that while in Italy he made inquiry about a dangerous band of outlaws and cutthroats that he had heard of in Italy. The man to whom he was speaking said: 'They have all gone to America.' . . . I protest against [this], Mr. President. I wish I had it in my power to shut these doors tight for at least twelve months' time."
>
> *Senator James Thomas Heflin, Alabama, speaking in the Senate in favor of limiting immigration in 1921*

▲ A statue of Italian American Marine John Basilone in Raritan, New Jersey. In 1942, Basilone became the first enlisted marine to be awarded the Medal of Honor in World War II. He also received the Navy Cross and Purple Heart. Basilone was killed in action in 1945.

"Enemy Aliens"

More ill feeling against Italians arose in the 1930s. Europe was in turmoil, and Benito Mussolini became dictator in Italy. He allied himself with Adolf Hitler, the Nazi leader of Germany, to fight the Allies in World War II. When the United States entered the war in 1941, Italy was an enemy nation, and Italian Americans were viewed with some distrust.

More than six hundred thousand Italian-born Americans, or resident aliens, were forced to register with the government as "enemy aliens." Some of these Italian Americans were told that they could only travel in certain areas of their home cities. About ten thousand Italian Americans were placed in internment camps. Fishermen on the West Coast lost their livelihoods because they were banned from going out to sea, where it was thought they might threaten national security. Entire coastal communities were ordered to leave their homes and live inland. Ironically, many of these people whose lives were destroyed—and whose rights were ignored—had sons fighting with the U.S. military in Europe and in the Pacific.

Conflict in the Family

In the 1930s and 1940s, internal conflict also hit some Italian American families. Italian Americans raised in the United States— like the children of other immigrant groups—wanted to become "American." Many felt as though they lived double lives—a largely Italian home life and a largely American lifestyle outside the home. They could become acutely embarrassed when their parents' words or actions in public made it obvious that they were Italian. One of these children later recalled, "We were becoming American by learning to be ashamed of our parents."

School could be a source of tension between the generations. Teachers felt the need to Americanize the children of immigrants.

▶ Like all other Americans, these Italian Americans took to the streets of their neighborhood to celebrate the end of World War II in 1945.

They taught them about U.S. history and government and how to speak English. Many parents worried that schools might undermine what they taught their children at home.

Younger Italian Americans often rebelled. Some wanted to continue their educations rather than start work. Others wanted to express their own wishes in the choice of who they should marry rather than leave that decision to their parents. Such challenges to the parents' authority produced conflict and bitter feelings on both sides.

Struggling with Different Attitudes

The immigrant Italian Americans were often hurt by the attitudes of their Americanized children. Novelist Lucas Longo wrote a novel in which an Italian American man becomes a doctor and changes his name from Bentolinardo to Bentley. The decision crushes his father, who laments, "Sick I went to work. With fever. I saved. Every penny. For him. My Ralph. And how does the traitor pay me back?" Although fictional, the story reflects the conflicts that split some families.

"Sometimes, in this generation gap, Italian boys especially, realizing their parents were dead wrong, became nastily indignant. That led to shouting matches in which the kids and the father, sometimes the mother, said terrible things to one another. Two or three of the boys I grew up with ran away and were never heard [from] again."

John Ciardi, Italian American poet and teacher, remembering life in the 1930s

▲ An Italian American policeman talks with members of his community in 1943. As Italian Americans became more accepted in U.S. society, their roles in the community changed, and they began to take on positions of authority.

"What they learned of this strange country often repelled them. From their perspective, the 'Mericani appeared a foolish people, without a sense of humor, respect, or proper behavior. Ideas of youthful freedom, women's rights, . . . they dismissed. . . . Efforts on the part of teachers and social workers to Americanize them and their children were resented as intrusions on the [rights] of the family."

Rudolph Vecoli,
Italian American historian

Many Italian American immigrants were not happy with what they knew of U.S. culture. A phrase heard in many Italian American homes was "*Mannagia LaMerica,*" or "Curse America." It expressed the immigrants' frustration with the foreign society in which they found themselves.

Changing Times

As Italian American children grew up and became adults, American Italian society changed. By the 1920s, many of the younger generations were able to get better jobs working in factories than had been possible in earlier years. As parents, these Italian Americans were able to let their children stay in school. Only in the late 1940s, however, did large numbers of Italian Americans begin to go to college. Many of the Italian Americans who did so were veterans of World War II who used the benefits of the G.I. Bill to fund their educations.

Over time, even the immigrant Italian Americans adapted to U.S. life. They scrimped and saved so they could move out of the tenement building and buy a little plot of land with a house. As soon as they did, many planted vegetable gardens that they tended with loving care. Some Italian Americans developed these plots of land into successful truck farms that supplied fresh produce to New York City and other urban areas.

As years passed, more Italian Americans became citizens and voted in elections. Beginning in the 1920s, Italian American politicians began to win important political positions. By the 1960s and 1970s, Italian Americans served in all levels of government. Among the most well-known was Fiorello LaGuardia, who was elected

Connecting with the Homeland

Italian Americans, like other immigrant groups, often sent money to their families in the homeland. Millions of dollars flowed back to Italy, helping prop up the poor economy of the southern regions. An Italian government report from the 1890s said, "the marked increase in the wealth in certain sections of Italy can be traced directly to money earned in the United States." Italian Americans, however, sometimes found that relatives in Italy had unreasonable expectations of how much money people were able to earn in the United States and wanted financial help that the Americans could not provide.

As years went by, some Italian Americans kept connections alive by returning to the old country to visit their families. These trips could be difficult. Years of life in the United States had changed the former immigrants, and they could no longer accept the traditional Italian life they rediscovered in Italy. Rosa Vartone returned to visit her mother thirty-three years after she had left. "Everything looked different to me," she later recalled, "because I got used to over here."

▲ Fiorello LaGuardia was the son of an Italian immigrant father and a Jewish mother who came from Austria-Hungary. He gained his greatest fame as mayor of New York City; one of the city's main airports is named after him. LaGuardia worked continuously to improve the lives of the poor, especially immigrants, and to fight crime and corruption.

mayor of New York City in 1933 and served three terms.

A New Kind of Italian American

The younger Italian American generations saw themselves in a different way from earlier generations. No longer was a person's sense of identity based on the original village or region. Instead, their bonds were with other Italian Americans as a group. These generations were more likely than their parents to marry partners who were not Italian Americans. They were also more likely to divorce, although Italian Americans still had lower divorce rates than Americans as a whole. As in other U.S. families, later generations tended to have fewer children than their parents.

The United States adapted to Italian Americans as well. The new immigration laws of the 1920s—along with the problems of the 1930s and World War II—slowed immigration from Italy, and other lands, to a trickle. As a result, nativist anger faded. Another reason for acceptance was growing familiarity. In many cities, children from other groups went to school with Italian American children. They found Italians pretty similar in tastes and interests. Men who fought in World War II with Italian American soldiers became more accepting of Italian Americans as a whole.

The popularity of the Italian American sports and entertainment figures who rose to fame in the 1940s gave a new image to Italian American society. New York Yankee Joe DiMaggio played baseball with grace and skill and became a national hero. Singer Frank Sinatra was idolized by millions of teenage girls across the country and became one of the United States' most enduring stars.

Waves of Immigrants Clash

One measure of the extent to which Italian Americans of the first wave adapted was how they got along with immigrants of the second wave—those that came after World War II. The two groups did not always mix well. Italian American Fred Gardaphe recalled that when one of these families moved next door to his own, the other family laughed at his mother's poor Italian—and he laughed at the newcomers' broken English. Over many years, however, his attitude changed. "The people next door brought me closer to my Italian heritage, but only after I realized that my idea of being American was falsely rooted in trying to distance myself from them."

Adaptation by Later Immigrants

Immigrants who arrived after World War II found it somewhat easier to adapt to U.S. life. The widespread prejudice that Italian Americans faced in the early 1900s was largely—although not entirely—a thing of the past. In addition, in a world of international trade and global communications, there were fewer barriers between Italian and U.S. cultures. Later Italian immigrants had often had some exposure to U.S. culture before they reached the United States. Of course, they still faced adjustments. Mario Lucci, who came to the United States as a child in 1972, recalled later that his mother was shocked to see American girls wearing miniskirts.

▶ In the later generations, Italian American children became more American than Italian. In Connecticut, students from different immigrant backgrounds, including Italian Americans, attended a school celebration in May 1942.

Italian Americans in U.S. Society

Today, almost seventeen million people call themselves Italian Americans. Estimates say another ten million people have at least one Italian American grandparent. These numbers exceed those of any European group except for German, Irish, and British.

Where They Live

Most Italian Americans live in the the states of the Northeast and Midwest, California, or Florida. New York, with almost three million, is the state with the highest number of Italian Americans. Rhode Island has the highest proportion of Italian Americans, however—almost 20 percent of its population. Connecticut and New Jersey have about the same proportion. Almost all Italian Americans

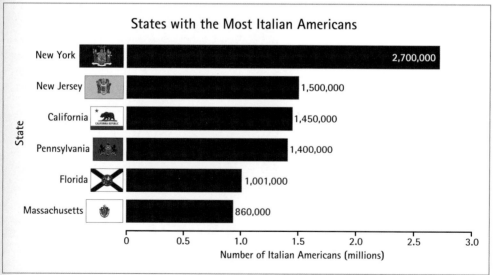

States with the Most Italian Americans

State	Number of Italian Americans
New York	2,700,000
New Jersey	1,500,000
California	1,450,000
Pennsylvania	1,400,000
Florida	1,001,000
Massachusetts	860,000

Number of Italian Americans (millions)

Source: U.S. Census Bureau, Census 2000

▲ Where Italian Americans live today reflects to some extent the pattern of settlement established long ago. This chart shows how many Italian Americans there were in the states with the largest Italian American populations in 2000.

—about nine out of every ten—live in cities or suburbs. The metropolitan regions around New York City; Philadelphia, Pennsylvania; Boston, Massachusetts; Chicago, Illinois; and Los Angeles and San Francisco in California have the largest Italian American populations in the nation.

Work and Education

In the past, a large number of Italian Americans worked in manufacturing. Today, about two-thirds of Italian Americans have jobs in service industries. This change reflects the way the U.S. economy has also changed. In 2000, the median family income—a fair guide of economic status—of Italian American families ($61,297 a year) was higher than the median income for U.S. families as a whole ($50,046).

In the early 1900s, Italian Americans were behind other groups in education. Today, the share of Italian Americans with a high-school diploma, a college degree, or an advanced degree is slightly higher than the proportion for the U.S. population in general.

"Being an Italian American to me is knowing that when times are down your elders always have your back. Whether they make you a hot bowl of pastina or give a few words of wisdom . . . you know that in the end everything is going to be all right. Being Italian American means appreciating the finer side of Italian cuisine, the legendary talents of Frank Sinatra, and the importance of family and friendship bonding, before you can tie your shoelaces. It's having that 'never give up' attitude that our ancestors had."

Joe Salvati, a student at Loyola College, Baltimore, Maryland, 2003

Being Italian American

Many Italian Americans have strong feelings of pride. They point to the achievements of Italians, who gave the world great works of art and beautiful buildings and cities. They also express great pride in what Italian Americans achieved in the United States.

Some Italian Americans find the strong sense of family to be stifling, while others find comfort in it. Some are bitter about the harsh way that many Italian immigrants were treated. Others resent what they see as offensive stereotypes of their group in the media.

Contributions of Italian Americans

Italian Americans have made many contributions to the United States. Musicians, artists, singers, and sports champions of Italian descent have brought generations of talent to the United States. Italian American laborers helped build bridges, highways, and subway systems and manufactured countless products. Farmers helped start the wine and produce industries of California.

Italian American Holidays

Today, festas are held in many towns and cities across the United States. Communities still celebrate the days traditional to their neighborhood or town. In addition, Italian Americans have long viewed Columbus Day as a holiday special to them but also worthy of the entire country's respect. In recent years, some Native American groups have protested the holding of Columbus Day parades because so many Native Americans died as a result of the coming of Europeans. Many Italian Americans feel that blaming Columbus for the treatment of Native Americans is unfair. They also do not want to see the end of Columbus Day celebrations.

▲ The *Festa del Giglio* has been held every July in Brooklyn, New York, since 1903. Italian Americans carry a huge structure—and band members—through the streets in a tradition from the village of Nola, Italy, which honors Saint Paulinus.

Some business people ran companies that were important locally and even nationally. Amadeo Pietro Giannini started a bank serving Italian immigrants and others in San Francisco. It became the Bank of America, one of the largest financial institutions in the country. Food processing companies such as Prince, Planters Peanuts, and Tropicana were launched by Italian Americans. Lee Iacocca won praise for helping rebuild the Chrysler Corporation automobile company during hard times in the 1970s.

Two of New York City's most well-known mayors, Fiorello LaGuardia and Rudolph Giuliani, were both Italian Americans. New York state also had two important Italian American governors, Al Smith—born Alfred Emanuele Ferrara—and Mario Cuomo. In 1928, Smith lost his bid to become the nation's first Italian American president. In 1984, Geraldine Ferraro became the first woman to win the nomination for vice president from a major political party. Many Italian Americans have served in Congress—about thirty were serving in 2005.

▲ Italian restaurants cluster in North Beach, an Italian American neighborhood in San Francisco, California.

A Piece of Italy in Every Home

Perhaps the most popular contribution made by Italian Americans to U.S. life is Italian food. Pasta and pizza are everyday foods for most Americans. Grilled sandwiches called *panini* are also popular, and so is the traditional cornmeal dish polenta. Every night, when faced with the decision of what to eat, millions of Americans choose Italian food. The fact that regional Italian dishes have become national staples is just one of many aspects of U.S. culture that reflect the role of Italian Americans in the United States.

Notable Italian Americans

Constantino Brumidi (1805–1880)
Painter who arrived around 1850 and
painted historical scenes on the walls
and ceilings of the U.S. Capitol in
Washington, D.C.

Mother Frances Xavier Cabrini
(1850–1917) Nun who came to New
York in 1889 and built hospitals,
orphanages, and schools. She was the
first American to be declared a saint.

Pascal D'Angelo (1894–1932) Writer
who came from southern Italy in
1910, wrote an acclaimed memoir,
Son of Italy, published in 1924, and
died in poverty at age thirty-eight.

Joe DiMaggio (1914–1999) U.S.-born
son of an immigrant fisherman who
became a star player for the New
York Yankees and in 1941 achieved
an unbeaten record of hitting safely
in fifty-six straight games.

Enrico Fermi (1901–1954) Brilliant
scientist and winner of the Nobel
Prize for Physics in 1938 who fled
to the United States from Mussolini's
rule and contributed to building the
first atomic bomb.

Amadeo Pietro Giannini
(1870–1949) U.S.-born son of Italian
immigrants who founded the Bank
of Italy, later the Bank of America,
in 1904; by the 1930s, it was the
largest U.S. bank.

Lee Iacocca (1924–) U.S.-born son
of an immigrant who led the Chrysler
Corporation away from collapse in
the late 1970s and led the restoration
of the Ellis Island immigration station
as a national monument.

Fiorello LaGuardia (1882–1947)
U.S.-born son of immigrants and
politician who served in Congress
for six terms and then as mayor of
New York City for twelve years from
1934 to 1945.

Frank Sinatra (1915–1998) U.S.-
born son of a Sicilian-born father and
Genoese mother who became one of
the world's most famous singers and
an Academy Award-winning actor.

Arturo Toscanini (1867–1957)
World-famous conductor who led the
New York Philharmonic Orchestra and
NBC Symphony Orchestra. He was
also known for his protests against
Mussolini's rule in Italy.

Rudolph Valentino (1895–1926)
Actor, born Rodolfo Guglielmi, who
came to the United States at age
eighteen and became one of the
first and most-adored movie stars
in the era of silent movies.

Time Line

1850 About thirty-five hundred Italians are living in the United States.

1861 Most of Italy is unified as one kingdom.

1865 Constantino Brumidi paints an image of George Washington on the ceiling of the Rotunda in the U.S. Capitol.

1880 The newspaper *Il Progresso Italo-Americano* is founded in New York City.

1881 Major wave of Italian immigration begins.

1885 Congress passes a law banning immigrant labor contracts in effort to end the padrone system.

1889 Mother Cabrini comes to the United States and begins her mission to help Italian immigrants.

1891 Eleven Italian Americans are brutally murdered by a mob in New Orleans, Louisiana.

1892 Ellis Island immigration station opens in New York Harbor.

1899 The U.S. Roman Catholic Church begins to introduce Italian parishes.

1904 A. P. Giannini starts the bank that later becomes the Bank of America.

1905 Order of the Sons of Italy is founded.

1917 Law requiring immigrants to pass a literacy test is enacted.

1917–1918 Thousands of Italian Americans fight for the United States in World War I.

1920 Nicola Sacco and Bartolomeo Vanzetti are arrested and tried; their case helps increase anti-immigrant feelings.

1921 Congress passes a law limiting immigration and putting quotas on numbers of immigrants from each country.

1924 National Origins Act (also called the Immigration Act of 1924) further limits immigration, ending the main wave of Italian immigration.

1928 Italian American Al Smith is defeated in his bid to win the U.S. presidency.

1933 Fiorello LaGuardia is first elected mayor of New York City.

1941 U.S. enters World War II as an enemy of Italy; during the war, hundreds of thousands of Italian Americans are classified as enemy aliens, while thousands of others fight with the U.S. military.

1946 Mother Cabrini is declared a saint by the Catholic Church.

1948 Displaced Persons Act allows four hundred thousand Italians and other refugees who suffered because of World War II to enter the United States.

1951–1970 Second wave of Italian immigration takes place.

1984 Geraldine Ferraro, a Democrat from New York, becomes the first woman to win nomination for vice president from a major political party.

1994 Rudolph Giuliani becomes mayor of New York City.

2003 Nancy Pelosi becomes Minority Leader of the House of Representatives and the highest-ranking Italian American in Congressional history.

Glossary

alien person living in a nation other than his or her birth nation and who has not become a citizen of his or her new nation of residence

census official population count

culture language, beliefs, customs, and ways of life shared by a group of people from the same region or nation

dialect local version of a language, with its own pronunciation and unique words, which is not always understood by people who speak different dialects of the same language

dowry money given by a bride's family to the family of the man she is marrying

emigrate leave one nation or region to go and live in another place

exile person who is forced or feels compelled to leave his or her homeland

extortion crime of taking money from people by using threats or force

fresco painting on a plaster surface, such as a wall or ceiling

G.I. Bill law passed in 1944 that gave low-cost housing loans and college loans to those who had served in the U.S. military during World War II

heritage something handed down from previous generations

immigrant person who arrives in a new nation or region to take up residence

internment camp place where people are confined, usually during wartime

literacy ability to read and write

median family income level of income at which half the population earns more and half earns less

mutual aid society organization in which members of the group, who are usually from a common background, help each other and perform social services separately from government agencies or private businesses

nativist person who wanted limits placed on U.S. immigration to protect the power and position of white, U.S.-born Americans

parish area served by a single church

patron saint Catholic saints who are named as having special protective powers over a village, region, or aspect of life

prejudice bias against or dislike of a person or group because of race, nationality, or other factors

quota assigned proportion; in the case of immigration, a limit on the number of immigrants allowed from a particular country

service industry area of work that provides services instead of products; service businesses include banks, entertainment, food service, tourism, and health care, among many others

steerage section of a steamship that provided poor accommodation and was used by passengers who could not afford cabins

stereotype an image, often incorrect, that people have of certain groups

tenement poorly built and crowded apartment buildings with bad ventilation and sanitation and low safety standards

truck farm farm growing fruit and vegetables to be sold at markets

Further Resources

Books

Anderson, Dale. *Arriving at Ellis Island*. Landmark Events in American History (series). World Almanac® Library (2002).

Creech, Sharon. *Granny Torrelli Makes Soup*. HarperTrophy (2005).

Hoobler, Dorothy, and Thomas Hoobler. *The Italian American Family Album*. American Family Albums (series). Oxford University Press (1998).

Murphy, Jim. *Pick and Shovel Poet: The Journeys of Pascal D'Angelo*. Clarion Books, 2000.

Web Sites

Ellis Island
www.historychannel.com/ellisisland/index2.html
Recreation of the Ellis Island experience from the History Channel

Milestones
www.niaf.org/milestones/index.asp
Milestones of the Italian American experience from the National Italian American Foundation

Publisher's note to educators and parents: Our editors have carefully reviewed these Web sites to ensure that they are suitable for children. Many Web sites change frequently, however, and we cannot guarantee that a site's future contents will continue to meet our high standards of quality and educational value. Be advised that children should be closely supervised whenever they access the Internet.

Where to Visit

Statue of Liberty Ellis Island National Monument
National Park Service, Liberty Island, New York, NY 10004
Telephone: (212) 363-3206; *www.nps.gov/stli/*

About the Author

Dale Anderson studied history and literature at Harvard University in Cambridge, Massachusetts. He lives in Newtown, Pennsylvania, where he writes and edits educational books. Anderson has written many books for young people, including a history of Ellis Island, published by World Almanac® Library in its *Landmark Events in American History* series.

Index